Tequila
Mockingbird

TEQUILA MOCKINGBIRD

COCKTAILS with a LITERARY TWIST

TIM FEDERLE

ILLUSTRATED BY

LAUREN MORTIMER

Running Press

PHILADELPHIA

© 2013 by Tim Federle
Illustrations © 2013 by Lauren Mortimer

Published by Running Press Book Publishers
An Imprint of Perseus Books, LLC.
A Subsidiary of Hachette Book Group, Inc.

Printed in China
RRD-S

Books published by Running Press are available at special discounts for bulk purchases in the United States by corporations, institutions, and other organizations. For more information, please contact the Special Markets Department at the Perseus Books Group, 2300 Chestnut Street, Suite 200, Philadelphia, PA 19103, or call (800) 810-4145, ext. 5000, or e-mail special.markets@perseusbooks.com.

ISBN 978-0-7624-4865-4
Library of Congress Control Number: 2012944541

E-book ISBN 978-0-7624-4876-0

2 9
Digit on the right indicates the number of this printing

Design by Joshua McDonnell
Edited by Jordana Tusman
Typography: Accanthis, Bembo, and Copperplate

Running Press Book Publishers
2300 Chestnut Street
Philadelphia, PA 19103-4371

www.runningpressbooks.com

For Brenda Bowen—worth her weight in Cuervo Gold

CONTENTS

Part 1

Part 2

INTRODUCTION

....

An English major walks into a bar . . .

Gentle Drinker:

Congrats. You fought through *War and Peace*, burned through *Fahrenheit 451*, and sailed through *Moby-Dick*. All right, all right, you nearly drowned in *Moby-Dick*, but you made it to shore—and you deserve a drink! Hang tight, undergrad. A beer's not going to cut it. Not this time.

To pay proper homage to the world's greatest stories and story-tellers, we've carefully crafted a library's worth of literature-inspired cocktails. Scholarly sips for word nerds, if you will—and the people who love them. From barflies to book clubs, welcome to *Tequila Mockingbird: Cocktails with a Literary Twist*. Go ahead and pull up a stool. Or a recliner, for that matter.

Don't worry if you snoozed your way through Comp Lit. Think of this recipe guide as SparkNotes with a liquor license, trading out pop quizzes for popped corks. For you serious drink-slingers out there, we're serving up your favorite recipes with a smart new twist. You've gotta have something to talk about behind the bar—why not raise the level of banter by brushing up on your Brontë?

There are beverages here to suit all tastes. Ladies, get ready to celebrate history's feistiest heroines in Drinks for Dames, a handful of recipes that take sugar and spice to a whole new level. From **Are You There God? It's Me, Margarita** to **A Rum of One's Own** to **Bridget Jones's Daiquiri**, we've got every reading level covered.

Gents, your brawny books go down easier with a halftime chug. In Gulps for Guys, literature's most savory stories get stirred into over two dozen recipes. From **The Last of the Mojitos** to **The Old Man and the Seagram's** and **Orange Julius Caesar**—with characters this vivid, you'll never drink alone again.

Book clubs, shake up your next gathering with party punches like **The Joy Luck Club Soda** and **The Pitcher of Dorian Grey Goose**. No problem if you haven't even read this month's selection—everyone's bound to be fall-down drunk, anyway. Just leave your keys by the door.

And fret not, recovering readers! We've got nonalcoholic drinks for you, too (**The Wonderful Blizzard of Oz**, anyone?) that recall gentler, less wobbly times. No shame in sitting back while the freshmen make fools of themselves.

If your buzz is on but your belly's empty, we've cooked up **The Deviled Egg Wears Prada, Prawn Quixote**, and a handful of other Bar Bites for Book Hounds. And should you find yourself surrounded by a group of hesitant readers—or card-carrying library-goers—try our drinking games. You'll be reading your friends under the table . . . you know, if they're brave enough to take a shot every time Dickens introduces a new character.

Relax. We won't get *too* stuffy. After all, the only things needed to enjoy a good book are a lamp and a place to sit. An effective cocktail should be just as easy. For those who don't know their Bloody Mary from their Mary Shelley, flip the page for a quick refresher on the tools, techniques, and terms used throughout this book. Trust us: if you've got a Solo cup and a corner store, you can make 90 percent of these recipes 100 percent of the time.

So grab a glass, already. Let's get a little stupid and look a little smart. Even if you *don't* have a BA in English, tonight you're gonna drink like you do.

TOOLS

GLASSWARE

Cocktail (or martini) glass (4 to 6 ounces): Drinks are shaken and strained into this long-stemmed, iconic *v*-shaped beauty.

Collins glass (10 to 14 ounces): Built like a highball glass, but taller and narrower. Best for icy, very large tropical drinks. Also best for getting drunk.

Flute (4 to 6 ounces): Champagne cocktails are served in this specially designed stemware, which showcases the bubbles without letting too many of them fly free.

Highball glass (10 to 12 ounces): Midway between a rocks and a Collins glass, but taller than the former and shorter and fatter than the latter. If you could only have one book on a desert island, you'd choose wisely; if you could only have one glass, you'd choose this.

Mason jar (1 cup to ½ gallon): Though generally used for bottling preserves, this also makes a great container for down-home, country drinks.

Mug (10 to 12 ounces): The hardworking coffee cup does double duty for hot alcoholic drinks.

Pint glass (16 to 20 ounces): An all-purpose beer-chugger, this glass tapers at the bottom, and some have a "bulb" near the lip for a better grip.

Rocks (or lowball or old-fashioned) glass (6 to 10 ounces): A drink poured "on the rocks"—that's over ice, rookie—is frequently served in one of these short, heavy tumblers.

Shot glass (¾ to 2 ounces): For ~~slamming back~~ calmly enjoying a variety of aptly named "shots." The smallest of drinking vessels, these are also handy as measuring devices.

Solo cup (16 ounces): A plastic red cup that is a typical dorm room and party staple. In a pinch, used for basically every drink ever.

EQUIPMENT

BLENDER: For frosty, feel-good frozen beverages. Make sure yours can handle ice like a champ.

JUICER: The classy crowd prefers their lemons and limes (and pomegranates, thank you very much) freshly juiced, whether by hand or by machine—but we won't balk if you go the bottled route. On average, lemons and limes produce about an ounce of juice each.

MEASURING CUPS AND SPOONS: Duh, right? Dry cups typically range from ¼ cup to 1 cup. For larger liquid measurements, it's easiest to have a standard 2-cup glass. Measuring spoons go from ¼ teaspoon to 1 tablespoon.

PITCHER AND PUNCH BOWL: Best for serving all the nonfiction characters in your life. Half-gallon pitchers always do the trick; same with a gallon punch bowl.

SHAKER: An essential device that need not intimidate! Our fave is the *Cobbler*: a three-part metal contraption (counting the capped lid) with the strainer built right in. The other varieties are the *Boston* (a glass mixing cup and metal container) and *French* (basically a *Cobbler* shaker sans strainer). Both require a separate strainer, and that's valuable time you could be reading—or drinking.

STRAINER: Like a sifter for liquids. If you ignored our advice to buy the all-in-one *Cobbler* shaker, you'll want to pick up a *Hawthorne* strainer, which will fit tight into your shaker's metal mouth. The *Hawthorne* filters only the liquids (not the ice) into a cocktail.

JIGGER: For small liquid measurements. A metal hourglass shape, available in a variety of sizes. We prefer the 1-ounce-over-1½-ounce model—but you should up the dosage if you're trying to get through *Anna Karenina*. And just drink straight from the bottle if you're attempting *Walden*.

MUDDLER: Grown-up term for fruit masher. Releases oils and flavors in mints and berries.

VEGETABLE PEELER (OR CHANNEL KNIFE): A handy shortcut for creating twists (see: Garnishes, page 8), the peeler removes a thin layer of skin from fruit to add flavor and color.

TECHNIQUES

....

MAKING A DRINK

FILLING: In some recipes, you're asked to "fill" your glass to the top with a final ingredient—typically Champagne, club soda, or cream. The amount of liquid needed depends on how large your glass is: from 2 to 4 ounces for a flute, to anywhere from 4 to 8 ounces for rocks, highball, or Collins glasses.

FLOATING: To create pretty layers in the drink, "float" one liquid on top of the other. The easiest method is to invert a spoon and slowly pour liquor/liqueur over the back of the head, letting the liquid pool without breaking the cocktail's surface—sort of like trying not to cry during *Of Mice and Men*.

ICING PUNCHES: For parties, blocks of ice are a cinch. Simply fill a clean, empty milk carton with water, freeze overnight, and peel away the waxy paper.

MUDDLING: In some recipes, once you've filled a glass with the specified fruits, juices, or herbs, use a *muddler* (page 6) to gently mash the ingredients, twisting lightly to release oils and flavors.

RIMMING: Rub the lip of the desired glass with a lemon or lime wedge, then "rim" the glass (hey, now!) by turning it upside down and placing the rim on a plate of salt, cocoa powder, sugar, or whatever the recipe calls for. Then gently rotate the glass so the rim gets coated in the desired ingredient.

SHAKING: Fill a *Cobbler* tin with all of the ingredients and ice, cap shut, and shake vigorously—harder than you think, bordering on "workout." Uncap the lid and strain into a glass.

STIRRING: Experts use a bar spoon, which has a long, twisting handle, but an everyday cereal spoon will do just fine. For cocktails with carbonation, the bubbles do the stirring for you.

DECORATING A DRINK

GARNISHES: Like a truly memorable book cover (remember the puppeteer's hand on *The Godfather*?), garnishes are the promise of something special to come. Technically, *garnish* adds both color and flavor (like a lime wedge or lemon twist), *garbage* is any food or fruit that's solely for aesthetic purposes (like a lemon wheel), and *kitsch* is something hokey (like an umbrella, or the entire plot of *Valley of the Dolls*).

Garnish techniques include:

TEARING: The easiest way to include mint in a cocktail. Simply wash, remove stems, and take out your frustration one rip at a time.

TWISTS: Delicately flavors a drink and adds a little citrus pizzazz. The official method involves a *channel knife*, which peels a long, thin gouge out of a lemon. Our easier, preferred method is to wash a lemon and then use a *vegetable peeler* to remove a 2-inch strip of skin. Fold in half, twist over drink, wipe the rim of the glass with the twist, and then drop into the glass.

WEDGES: The most widely seen lemon or lime garnish. Wash, dry, and cut the ends off the whole fruit. Then chop the fruit in half "the short way" and quarter the remaining halves. Wedges can either be squeezed and dropped into the drink, or balanced on the rim after cutting a notch into the fruit.

WHEELS: Circular discs of fruits or vegetables. Wash, dry, and cut the ends off the whole fruit, then slice crosswise into "wheels." Can be placed in the drink, or balanced on the rim after cutting a notch into the fruit.

TERMS

....

SPIRITS

GIN: Distilled from grain and, though flavored with everything from juniper to cinnamon, smells a bit like rubbing alcohol—but in a fun way. Favored by Fitzgerald.

RUM: Hemingway's main hooch is the best sugar-water money can buy. The lightest kinds are the youngest; the darkest can be older than seven years.

TEQUILA: Comes from the blue agave plant, not the cactus. The word "tequila" itself refers to a very specific region in Mexico, and the authentic stuff doesn't harbor any wayward worms. Kerouac adored it.

VODKA: Odorless and clear, vodka is typically distilled from potatoes and grains. Russians drink it straight, but Americans mix it up—William S. Burroughs in particular.

WHISKEY: Distilled from grains and hailing from America, Canada, Ireland, or Scotland. Dorothy Parker's prized drink is serious stuff by its lonesome, but it plays nice with others. We feature both rye whiskey and bourbon, which is any good Southerner's definition of whiskey.

LIQUEURS

Strong, syrupy spirits that are flavored any number of ways, from fruits to flowers; also includes schnapps. The following liqueurs make appearances throughout: *absinthe* and *ouzo* (licorice-like flavor), *amaretto* (almond/apricot flavor), *anise* (brands like Galliano and Herbsaint), *blackberry, butterscotch, cinnamon* (a brand like Goldschläger), *coffee* (a brand like Kahlúa), *crème de cassis* (blackcurrant flavor), *crème de menthe* (mint flavor), *elderflower* (a brand like St-Germain), *gin* (a brand like Pimm's), *hazelnut* (a brand like Frangelico), *limoncello* (lemon flavor) *melon, orange* (generics like triple sec and Curaçao; a brand like Grand Marnier), *peach schnapps*, and *sour apple schnapps.*

BEER

A malt brew and a hoppy flavor. Recipes in this book focus on lagers, specifically light beer and—good luck here—malt liquor.

WINE

Fermented juice from myriad fruits and grapes. In subcategories, we feature: *brandy*, generally a distillation of wine or fruit juice; *sweet vermouth*, a fortified wine flavored with herbs; *sherry*, a brightly sweet fortified wine hailing from Spain; and *Champagne*, a sparkling white wine from a specific French region.

OTHER FLAVORINGS

AGAVE NECTAR: A widely available sweetener, it goes down like honey with an exotic accent.

BITTERS: The cologne of cocktails, added in small amounts to give a drink depth and nuance. *Angostura* and *Peychaud's* are the two aromatic bitters featured in this book. The latter is a slightly sweeter, fruitier version of the former, and both are strong and majestic. We also use *orange bitters*, any brand of which will showcase a bright citrus flavor.

COARSE AND SEA SALT: The rough, grainy seasoning favored by foodies.

COCONUT CREAM: A bottled, sweetened coconut product (a brand like Coco Reál Cream of Coconut) for tropical drinks.

GRENADINE: A sweet red syrup that's a snap to make, and loads better than the corporate high-fructose junk sold to bars.

GRENADINE SYRUP

Boil 2 cups bottled pomegranate juice (a brand like POM Wonderful) with 2 cups granulated sugar in a medium saucepan. Stir for 5 minutes, until it's reduced to half the original volume, into a syrup. Bottle and keep in the fridge for months. Or days, if you party like us.

HOT SAUCE: Available in any number of brands, all featuring a peppery kick.

ORGEAT: A sweet syrup made from almonds, sugar, and orange.

WASABI PASTE: A Japanese condiment—you've seen it next to sushi—that goes down hotter than *Lady Chatterley's Lover*.

WORCESTERSHIRE SAUCE: Contains everything from anchovies to molasses, and adds a steak-sauce slurp to certain cocktails.

THIRSTY YET? THESE DRINKS AREN'T GOING TO MAKE THEMSELVES.

1

DRINKS FOR DAMES

> "I like to have a martini,
>   Two at the very most.
>   After three I'm under the table,
>   After four I'm under my host."
>   —Dorothy Parker

Every night is ladies' night in this section, but it ain't all chick lit—
not that there's anything wrong with that. Yesteryear's heroines
may have been buttoned up to their Victorian eyeballs, but we're
rolling up our sleeves for a group of drinks as tart and tasty as the
trailblazing leading ladies who inspired them. Featuring English
feminists, demonic teens, and wicked nurses, the following recipes
are worth a sinful sip. Books down and bottoms up!

ONE FLEW OVER THE

COSMO'S NEST

ONE FLEW OVER THE CUCKOO'S NEST (1962)
BY KEN KESEY

K esey's groundbreaking novel, written while he was a student at Stanford, was drawn from his stint as a psych ward employee—when he wasn't volunteering in LSD "trials" on the side. (The late fifties weren't all *Leave It to Beaver*, gang.) Though narrated by a paranoid side-character, the hero of the story is McMurphy (Jack Nicholson in the firecracker film version), who leads his fellow mental patients in a rebellion against Nurse Ratched, a needle-wielding vixen who represents the tyranny of society—and seriously raises the question "Who's the *real* crazy here?" Liberate your own hemmed-in ways with a Cosmo you'd be cuckoo to pass on.

1½ ounces vodka
1 ounce cranberry juice
½ ounce triple sec
½ ounce lime juice

Combine the ingredients with ice in a shaker. Shake well and strain into a chilled cocktail glass. Code blue: it's hard to stop at just one of these—especially if all the other voices in your head are parched, too.

ETHAN POM

ETHAN FROME (1911)
BY EDITH WHARTON

T alk about a tough winter: Edith Wharton packed this one full of snowstorms, adultery, and—anyone for sledding?—a full-on suicide mission, headfirst into a tree. We reckon that if tragic hero Ethan, tragic zero Zeena, and merry mistress Mattie had been alive during the self-help era, they could've worked out that love triangle in an old-fashioned, nationally televised quarrel. But don't call us prudes—if they'd had a lick (or two) of our snowscape-inspired *Ethan Pom* slushy, who knows? They might have giggled their way into literature's first thruple.

> 3 ounces Champagne
> 3 ounces grenadine syrup (page 11)

Pour the Champagne into a rocks glass and then pack with shaved or crushed ice. Drizzle the syrup on top. Now, go for a stroll through town with your most cherished partner-in-crime. (Just don't let your boyfriend find out.)

RYE AND PREJUDICE

PRIDE AND PREJUDICE (1813)
BY JANE AUSTEN

Austen's frothy nineteenth-century masterpiece, which brought the author little acclaim during her short lifetime ("Forty-one is the new dead," sadly), follows a family's efforts to marry off its five daughters, one of whom leads the narrative. Unfortunately, Elizabeth—famously played onscreen by Keira Knightley's cheekbones—has a judgy streak that practically overshadows the love she has for Mr. Darcy, a stuck-up (but rich!) gentleman. Not to worry: there's a delectable double wedding in the end. We match-make two strong personalities—spicy rye and zingy grapefruit—for an unexpected marriage that'll get folks drinking, dancing, and dropping old judgments.

> 3 ounces grapefruit juice
> 1½ ounces rye whiskey

Pour the ingredients over ice in a rocks glass, stirring like a complicated heart. We hold no prejudice against marrying up, ladies, but you don't need a castle (or a king) to be a queen.

LOVE IN THE TIME OF KAHLÚA

LOVE IN THE TIME OF CHOLERA (1985)
BY GABRIEL GARCÍA MÁRQUEZ

Never settle . . . even for a doctor . . . with a hot accent. Otherwise, you could go a half-century till you find the real thing. In Márquez's version of romance, the zipper-straining desire of a trio of lovebirds is practically an illness, eating his characters from the inside out. Here, two teenagers fall in lust, but the girl chooses an MD to settle down with, leaving the boy to choose anything with two legs to settle the score. True adoration knows no calendar, and "fifty-one years, nine months and four days" later (but who's counting?), the two are reunited again after Husband the First dies. Adored as a Colombian treasure, this book deserves a nod that's as sweet as love and as spicy as lust.

> 1 ounce light rum
> ½ ounce coffee liqueur (like Kahlúa)
> 2 ounces light cream
> Ground cinnamon or nutmeg, to taste

Combine the rum and coffee liqueur over ice in a rocks glass. Pour the cream on top and sprinkle a little spice. Now, drink to the heady brew of passion—even if the only foreign doctor in your life is on TV.

BRAVE NEW SWIRLED

BRAVE NEW WORLD (1932)
BY ALDOUS HUXLEY

I magine a world dominated by antidepressants and governmental control over reproductive rights. (Oh. Wait.) Written in the thirties, *Brave New World* could've been copy-and-pasted from today's headlines. Huxley penned a dystopian world in which embryos are preprogrammed for certain behaviors and needs, and technology is so revered that "Oh my Ford" is a commonplace utterance. While Huxley was an outspoken fan of psychedelic drugs, you can *legally* freeze your own brain with a swirly smoothie featuring a surprising aphrodisiac: watermelon. Hey, what you drink (and who you drink it with) ain't nobody's business but your own.

  1 ounce vodka
  1 cup seedless watermelon, chopped into coarse cubes
  ¼ ounce lemon juice
  ½ teaspoon granulated sugar
  ½ ounce melon liqueur

Add the vodka, watermelon, lemon juice, sugar, and a handful of ice to a blender, running until smooth. Pour into a cocktail glass and float the liqueur on top. No matter your political leanings, one gulp of this and you'll be more than brave enough to fight The Man.

A COCKTAIL OF TWO CITIES

A TALE OF TWO CITIES (1859)

BY CHARLES DICKENS

For readers of *All the Year Round*, a weekly journal that Charles Dickens published himself, it took over thirty issues to tell a tale set between Paris and London during the French Revolution. Though the cities are the real stars, there's a tragically romantic love story that plays out on their streets, starring a golden-haired beauty and the two men who are willing to die for her (talk about "the best of times"). Toast to sooty chivalry with our take on a famous drink that hails from "The New York Bar" in Paris: a Cocktail of Two Cities that requires nary a passport.

1 sugar cube
1 ounce gin
½ ounce lemon juice
Champagne, to fill

Place the sugar cube in a flute. Pour the gin and lemon juice into a shaker with ice, and shake well. Strain into the flute. Fill to the top with Champagne. The result is *revolutionary*.

THE COOLER PURPLE

THE COLOR PURPLE (1982)
BY ALICE WALKER

This winner of both a National Book Award *and* a Pulitzer inspired a movie *and* a musical for its depiction of black southern life in the first half of the twentieth century. Alice Walker tells her novel in letters, first from a fourteen-year-old Celie, spilling her confusion to God, and later between a maturing Celie and her sister, whose correspondence from Africa highlights similar racial woes back home in Georgia. A modern classic, *The Color Purple* blooms bright for anyone willing to face its painful beauty. Cool off an oppressively warm night with a sweetly hued shot, pondering how far our world has come—and how much further we've got to go.

½ ounce blackberry liqueur
½ ounce peach schnapps
½ ounce light rum
½ ounce lemon juice

Combine the ingredients in a shaker with ice and shake well. Strain into a shot glass. Alternatively, double the recipe and invite your sister over. Nothing bonds as fast as booze.

FRANGELICO AND ZOOEY

FRANNY AND ZOOEY (1961)
BY J. D. SALINGER

A cat named Bloomberg, a dude named Zooey, and a girl who smokes in the tub: we spy hipsters! Originally appearing in two *New Yorker* installments as part of a larger series about the Glass family, J. D. Salinger's *Franny and Zooey* concerns a college coed who is so at wit's end with campus poseurs and politics, she faints while at a restaurant with her boyfriend. He flees—hell, there's a football game—and Franny's left chanting a prayer, all by her kooky lonesome. With a religious wink to Frangelico, the nutty liqueur in a monk-shaped bottle, find your center by icing down those troubles over some decaf.

2 ounces decaf espresso, chilled
1 ounce hazelnut liqueur (like Frangelico)
2 ounces light cream

Put on a cardigan, a jazz album, and a frown. Then pour the espresso and liqueur over ice in a rocks glass, adding the cream on top. Not smiling yet? For the love of Brooklyn, be thankful you've got this much time—and this little responsibility—to feel so full of angst. It won't last forever, baby!

BLOODY CARRIE

CARRIE (1974)

BY STEPHEN KING

Children can be so cruel. Sixteen-year-old Carrie White is already a social outcast when she adds every girl's nightmare to the list: having her first period in a gym class *shower*. It gets messier from there, with scheming teens setting Carrie up to win prom queen, only to crown her not with a tiara, but—can't get *this* at Walmart—with pig's blood. Little do her fellow classmates know about Carrie's secret telekinetic powers (it's a Stephen King novel after all, his first to get published), and our heroine buttons the novel with a fair impression of Satan going through puberty. Spice up a legendary drink with ingredients even a schoolgirl has on hand—though there's no way you're serving this one virgin.

5 ounces tomato juice

2 ounces vodka

½ ounce lime juice

½ teaspoon Worcestershire sauce

¼ teaspoon wasabi paste

3 dashes hot sauce

Salt and pepper, to taste

Add the ingredients to a shaker with ice. Shake well and strain over fresh ice in a Collins glass. Traditionalists would finish with a celery stalk, but if you're a gal who likes to stir *trouble* instead of drinks, you'll be too busy doubling the wasabi.

HOWARDS BLEND

HOWARDS END (1910)

BY E. M. FORSTER

S ad that the writer of "Only connect"—*Howards End*'s epi-
graph—had such a tortured time doing so himself. Edward
Morgan (E. M.) Forster, the long-closeted novelist of the literary
masterpieces *A Room with a View* and *A Passage to India* (the last
book he'd write for fifty years, until his death), imagined three distinct families in *Howards End*, an English estate at the center of
class tensions, inheritance resentments, and the rare death-by-
falling-bookcase. Here, we blend the three distinct flavors of the
vintage "Janet Howard" cocktail, for a posh but pronto drink.
This'll have you connecting in no time—with other people, God
willing, not toppled furniture.

   2 ounces brandy
   ½ ounce orgeat syrup
   2 dashes Angostura bitters

A perfect drink for the day you receive word your wealthiest
relative has finally ~~kicked the bucket~~ passed on. Shake the
ingredients with ice and strain into a cocktail glass—and
gather the bravery to ask if you were left anything in the will.

GIN EYRE

JANE EYRE (1847)
BY CHARLOTTE BRONTË

You know what's too tragic to be funny? A feminist survivor story published under a male pseudonym. With Charlotte Brontë writing as Currer Bell, *Jane Eyre* (think: Gloria Steinem in a bonnet) is the retrospective of an abused orphan-child turned bored teacher-girl turned lovesick governess-lady. Unfortunately, her groom already has a wife—Brontë didn't give the heroine any breaks—and Jane sets off on a soul-quest, refusing subsequent marriage proposals and eventually landing the man, the baby, and the happy home. Brontë wasn't so lucky; she died while pregnant, less than ten years after *Jane* debuted to acclaim. Raise a glass of English gin to a legendary lady, worthy of a sweeter finish than befell her.

8 sprigs fresh mint, washed
2 ounces English gin
1 ounce lemon juice
1½ teaspoons granulated sugar
2 dashes orange bitters

Add the ingredients to a shaker with ice, with bonus points if you tear the mint leaves first. Shake well and strain into a cocktail glass. Now nurse that drink like a good nanny.

PARADISE SAUCED

PARADISE LOST (1667)

BY JOHN MILTON

An apple a day may keep the dentist away, but the Devil's no doctor. *Paradise Lost*, Milton's seventeenth-century blank verse poem (don't hold your breath for Dr. Seuss rhymes), was one of the first examples of Christian literature to paint Adam, Eve, and even your old friend Satan in gray strokes—it's less good vs. evil than complicated vs. conflicted. Remarkably, Milton didn't just *write* a twelve-part book, he *spoke* it: the author was blind, so he had to dictate the entire text to some kind of angel. Toast Milton's Godlike effort with a recipe that features a sinful apple at its core. It'll be worth the price tomorrow morning.

Sugar, for cocktail rim (page 7)
1½ ounces vodka
1 ounce sour apple schnapps
½ ounce lime juice
½ teaspoon granulated sugar

Rim a chilled cocktail glass in sugar and set aside. Shake the ingredients with ice and strain into the glass. You don't need a man to enjoy life's splendors, but prepare to pucker up after a sip of this sour sauce.

THE JOY OF SEX ON THE BEACH

THE JOY OF SEX (1972)
BY ALEX COMFORT

Keep a legend around long enough and it eventually comes (*ahem*) back into style. Such is the case with *The Joy of Sex*, a cheeky (literally) seventies how-to guide that was modeled after cookbooks, subbing out ears of corn with ears of people. The original pencil drawings—featuring shaggy-haired, mustached men exchanging coital maneuvers with what appeared to be a grown-up Marcia Brady—have in recent years been expanded upon, fully fleshed out, and updated with all new terms (now introducing: STDs!). Bottom line? This book took the science out of sex and injected it with feel-great fun. Here, we offer our own position on the standby cocktail. Have a ball—and do sip safe.

    2 ounces pineapple juice
    1 ounce vodka
    1 ounce peach schnapps
    1 (12-ounce) can lemon-lime soda

Combine the pineapple juice, vodka, and schnapps in a shaker with ice. Shake well and strain over fresh ice in a highball glass. Fill to the top with the lemon-lime soda. Alternatively? Combine the ingredients, freeze in an ice cube tray, and then add a hot partner to the mix.

A MIDSUMMER NIGHT'S BEAM

A MIDSUMMER NIGHT'S DREAM (CIRCA 1600)
BY WILLIAM SHAKESPEARE

Take two parts Ren Faire and one part Greek mythology, add a liberal dash of forest-dwelling nymphs, and you've got Shakespeare's whimsical meditation on love and lunacy. An amateur might toast this oft-produced play with two melatonin and a gulp of cough syrup, but Lord, only a foolish mortal would try that—this is a dream, not a blackout. You'll want to stay upright, if drowsily so, for a light, vegetation-heavy drink that will keep you skimming all five acts before a proper fairy-blessed slumber. You might just wake up in love.

    8 sprigs fresh mint, washed
    ½ ounce lime juice
    2 teaspoons granulated sugar
    2 ounces bourbon (like Jim Beam)
    1 (12-ounce) can club soda

Muddle the mint, lime juice, and sugar in a highball glass. Add ice and bourbon, and fill to the top with the club soda. Sip to your imagination's content—stopping only if your shadow begins to speak.

THE POSTMAN ALWAYS

BRINGS ICE

THE POSTMAN ALWAYS RINGS TWICE (1934)
BY JAMES M. CAIN

Neither snow nor rain nor heat nor gloom of night can keep two scheming lovers apart. In James M. Cain's noir novella, a drifter falls hard for a local lass with a dangerous pout and a body for sin. Trouble is, the drifter's new boss happens to be his new girlfriend's current *husband*, dubbed The Greek. You'll go postal for two-timing murders, killer dialogue, and S&M chatter that can still steam up an e-reader screen. Pair it with our bubbly Greek cocktail and you've got yourself a first-class package.

1 ounce ouzo
1 (12-ounce) can cola

Pour the ouzo over ice in a highball glass and fill to the top with the cola. Yes, those *are* bells you're hearing.

REMEMBRANCE OF
THINGS PABST

REMEMBRANCE OF THINGS PAST (1913–1927)
BY MARCEL PROUST

If at first you don't succeed, try submitting your 1.5-million-word manuscript again. Such was the fate of Proust's monumental seven-volume novel (which might as well have been called *Remembrance of Literally Everything Past*), initially rejected by publishers who are now kicking themselves in the grave. A thoughtful exploration on the tricky nature of time-telling, one passage has gained particular fame: Proust's narrator describes his sudden transportation back to childhood after tasting a madeleine soaked in tea. Take a journey to simpler times with a delicate summer drink that'll have you recalling your first secret sips of beer. And pair this drink with as many cookies as your memory demands.

6 ounces iced tea (Earl Grey is best)
1 (12-ounce) can beer (like Pabst Blue Ribbon)
1 lemon wedge, for garnish

Pour the iced tea into a pint glass and fill to the top with the beer, squeezing and dropping the lemon wedge into the glass. Now, kick back on a hammock, toss back a few madeleines, and pull out those old journals—or start a new one. (Beginner bloggers, just remember: the Internet is forever.)

BRIDGET JONES'S DAIQUIRI

BRIDGET JONES'S DIARY (1996)
BY HELEN FIELDING

S o what constitutes a classic, anyway? *We* say anything that gets people reading, sharing, and, in the case of *Bridget Jones's Diary*—a British smash turned international vacation read turned swoon-worthy movie—belly laughing. Reading just like your own diary, only with double the cigarettes and half the men (we're being nice), Bridget tells her *Pride and Prejudice*-inspired tale as a thirty-something singleton on the prototypical quest for real love—and a smaller dress size. With a nod to her ongoing list of New Year's resolutions, we go bubbly with a relatively low-cal daiquiri that even Bridget would enjoy. Do your duty and have one for her.

½ cup large, fresh strawberries (about 4), washed
1½ ounces Champagne
½ ounce lemon juice
½ teaspoon granulated sugar

Remove the greens from the strawberries—this is a drink, not a *salad*—and combine them in a blender with the Champagne, lemon juice, sugar, and a handful of ice. Blend until smooth and serve in a cocktail glass. And now? Take a sip of courage and let's finally create that online dating profile.

ROMEO AND JULEP

ROMEO AND JULIET (CIRCA 1599)
BY WILLIAM SHAKESPEARE

With the play's original title sounding like Shakespearean surfer slang—*The Most Excellent and Lamentable Tragedy of Romeo and Juliet*—this melancholy romance is for anyone who has fallen in love with the hot boy from the other side of the tracks. Who *can't* relate to the star-crossed lovers, doomed from the start by parents who, like, just don't understand? With a tragic, poisonous finale, this historic work created the mold, inspiring not only adaptations (*West Side Story* is just *R and J* with Puerto Rican accents and jazz hands), but also an entire road map for young-love stories. Fall under the spell of a drink so spring-like and peach-fuzzy, you might be forgiven for not realizing its full effects.

    6 sprigs fresh mint, washed
    1 teaspoon light brown sugar
    ½ ounce peach schnapps
    1½ ounces bourbon
    1 (12-ounce) can lemon-lime soda

In a highball glass, muddle the mint, sugar, and schnapps until the sugar dissolves like a relationship over summer break. Add ice and bourbon, and fill to the top with the lemon-lime soda. Prepare to fall in love—fast.

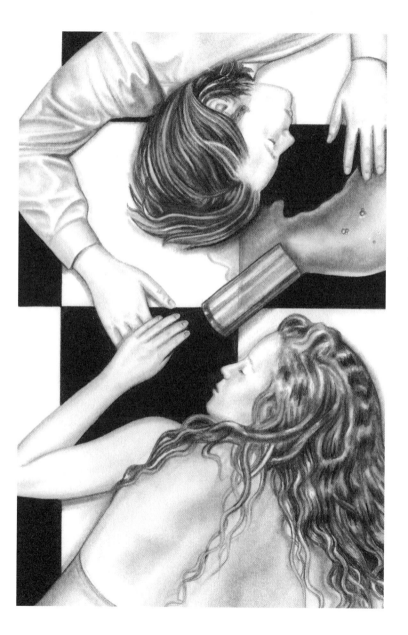

THE S(IDE)CARLET LETTER

THE SCARLET LETTER (1850)
BY NATHANIEL HAWTHORNE

Believe it or not, kiddos, there was a time when having a child out of wedlock wouldn't get you a reality show, but instead, a very public haranguing. In Hawthorne's *Scarlet Letter*—named after the "A for adultery" badge of dishonor the leading lady has to wear after birthing a bastard—Puritan New England serves as the case study of a world at odds with religion, hypocrisy, and desire. We push a drink purist's envelope by popping a few cherries (hey, now!) into a sweet and sour standby. This sidecar's so tasty, you might end up parading through town afterward, just like the heroine herself. Have no shame: this baby's all yours.

Sugar, for cocktail rim (page 7)
1 ounce cherry juice
½ ounce brandy
½ ounce triple sec

Rim a chilled cocktail glass in sugar and place aside. Shake the ingredients with ice and strain into the glass. You'll give this one a grade A.

A RUM OF ONE'S OWN

A ROOM OF ONE'S OWN (1929)
BY VIRGINIA WOOLF

Oh, Virginia. So smart. So sad. So ... specific. According to our gray Woolf, a woman needs "money and a room of her own if she is to write fiction." (She says nothing of *non*fiction, so apparently you can be broke and living with three other girls in a studio apartment if you're going the journalistic route.) We couldn't agree more with Ginny's recipe for storytelling success, though we'd add another thing to the list: a nice warm cocktail. Prepare the following bevvy on a writerly, wintery night. Who needs a man around with a drink this hot?

½ tablespoon salted butter, at room temperature
1 teaspoon light brown sugar
¼ teaspoon ground cinnamon
2 ounces dark rum

Place the butter, sugar, and cinnamon at the bottom of a mug and mix well with a metal spoon. Pour in the rum and fill to the top with hot water, then stir. And now? A long walk by the creek. No stone-collecting allowed.

TEQUILA MOCKINGBIRD

TO KILL A MOCKINGBIRD (1960)
BY HARPER LEE

All one-hit wonders should hit so hard! Harper Lee's only novel is the oft-taught tale told by little Scout Finch, watching her Alabama town rally behind a lying drunk's lying daughter, who's up and accused an innocent African-American man of taking advantage of her. Lucky for Scout—who watches from a courtroom balcony as her lawyer father defends the man—she's got levelheaded pals by her side, including Dill, who is famously modeled after Truman Capote. After a conclusion that leaves you both hopeful and haunted, toast to a sometimes sour justice system with a tequila shot that's guilty of packing a dill pickle punch.

1½ ounces tequila
2 drops hot sauce
1 dill pickle

Pour the tequila into a shot glass, add the hot sauce, and slam that bad boy back before chasing with a big chomp of pickle. No tears allowed here: if you can't stand the heat, get out of the South.

THE YELLOW WALLBANGER

"THE YELLOW WALLPAPER" (1892)
BY CHARLOTTE PERKINS GILMAN

Not recommended for our readers dwelling in studio apartments: Gilman's classic feminist short story traces one woman's descent into madness, locked in a bedroom by her physician husband as a cure for her vague hysterics. (See? Even in the 1800s, guys were writing girls off as crazy.) The hubby's plan backfires when the wifey grows nuttier and nuttier, becoming convinced that her makeshift prison cell's yellow wallpaper has somehow trapped other women within. We go bonkers for a recipe that's lasted the ages: bright as a yellow sun and sure to get you out of bed.

1½ ounces vodka
4 ounces orange juice
½ ounce Galliano liqueur

Combine the vodka and orange juice over ice in a highball glass. Give it a stir. Pour the Galliano on top, letting it stay just barely afloat—sort of like your sanity after one (or more) of these.

THE UNBEARABLE
LIGHTNESS OF PEEING

THE UNBEARABLE LIGHTNESS OF BEING (1984)
BY MILAN KUNDERA

C zech writer Kundera sets up this Communist-era classic with an open question about the paralyzing ramifications of our seemingly inconsequential everyday decisions. (Something tells us he didn't get invited to a lot of cocktail parties.) Kundera goes on to introduce a horndog surgeon with an impressive mistress-to-marriage ratio, but don't get too turned on! In the end, everybody ends up either dead or dejected, and you might be left questioning what your life would've looked like had you never picked up this meditation on politics and sex. Modify your mood with Prague's favorite spirit, at least for tourists. This quenching gulp goes down so much lighter than its namesake book that you'll be running to the bathroom after a few serious slurps.

3½ ounces pineapple juice
1 ounce absinthe
Lemon wheel, for garnish

Combine the ingredients over crushed ice in a rocks glass and garnish with the lemon wheel. Go soft pouring the (highly alcoholic) absinthe, lest you wake up contemplating where the hell you are.

ARE YOU THERE GOD?
IT'S ME, MARGARITA.

ARE YOU THERE GOD? IT'S ME, MARGARET. (1970)
BY JUDY BLUME

Move over, wizards. Make room, vampires. For many of us, Margaret was the original YA superstar, even if her epic battles were of the religion-and-puberty kind. (Actually, *especially* because of that.) Point is, Margaret showed us how to face all of life's big ol' quandaries, from God to boys to bra size. Ninety bucks says when Maggie got to college, she faced an even headier question: how the hell do you make a margarita without a blender? (Hint: on the rocks, kid.) Don't worry, Madges of the world, we've got your back. We'll even hold your hair when you've had one too many.

> Coarse salt, for cocktail rim (page 7)
> 1½ ounces tequila
> 1 ounce lime juice
> ½ ounce triple sec
> 1 lime wedge, for garnish (optional)

Rim a Solo cup in coarse salt and set aside. Dump all your feelings—er, *ingredients*—into a shaker with ice. Shake well and strain over fresh ice into the salted Solo cup. Or, if you're feeling classy, strain into a cocktail glass and garnish with a lime wedge. This is in Judy Blume's honor, after all.

THE **TURN** OF THE **SCREWDRIVER**

THE TURN OF THE SCREW (1898)
BY HENRY JAMES

O n a rolling country estate—the kind that always wins set designers their fifth Oscar—things are getting spooky for the new governess. In prolific author Henry James's novella, ghosts are after the new hire's charges, and she's determined to keep the tykes safe. Trouble is, nobody else seems to *see* these tricky apparitions, and more than a century after publication, even literary scholars are still scratching their heads: was the governess a lunatic, or was this a real haunted house? A true classic holds up to different interpretations, and we offer two ways into the Screwdriver—giving you twice the opportunity to check for ghosts in the bar.

Theory 1: She's perfectly levelheaded.
4 ounces orange juice
2 ounces vodka

Theory 2: She's batshit nuts.
4 ounces sparkling orange soda (like Orangina)
2 ounces vanilla vodka

For either variation, pour the ingredients over ice in a highball glass. If drinking alone, this may be better enjoyed in a plastic tumbler—just in case someone (or something) sneaks up behind you.

GULPS FOR GUYS

> "I work until beer o'clock."
> —Stephen King

Belly up to the bookcase, boys. It's time to brush up on the basics with a trip back down Hemingway lane. The following top-shelf gentlemen's classics are a diverse lot, starring soldiers, spies, and a *ton* of sailors. No, seriously: half of all literary masterpieces feature a fisherman with a grudge. And speaking of demons: ever notice how many famous male authors picked up the bottle as often as the pen? (We're looking at you, Faulkner. Step away from the gin, Fitzgerald.) Best to take these drinks one at a time, then. They deserve to be lingered over, just like your favorite novel.

CRIME AND PUNISH-MINT

CRIME AND PUNISHMENT (1866)
BY FYODOR DOSTOYEVSKY

W hen the lead character compares himself *favorably* to Napoleon, you turn off the laugh track on page one. New readers of *Crime and Punishment*—the tortured tale of a man who feels destined to murder a pawnbroker and then redistribute the wealth—might think they're tuning in for a literary *Law & Order*. Those readers are wrong. Crime? Sure! But punishment? Forget primetime courtroom scenes, because the only punishment here is the murderer's life sentence of guilt. Pair Russia's homeland brew—vodka, baby!—with just enough caffeine to give you the shakes. The mint should calm your nerves before you do anything *too* crazy.

1½ ounces vodka
½ ounce coffee liqueur
½ ounce crème de menthe liqueur
Light cream, to fill

Pour the vodka and liqueurs over ice in a rocks glass. Fill to the top with light cream—or heavy. Hey, you only live once.

DECLINE AND FALL DOWN

DECLINE AND FALL (1928)

BY EVELYN WAUGH

Don't worry, we're not gonna get all moralist on your ass (you're thinking of *The History of the Decline and Fall of the Roman Empire*, six volumes through which you dutifully texted). No, this is the breezily English satire *Decline and Fall*, Evelyn Waugh's delicious take on university life. Meet Paul Pennyfeather: booted out of Oxford for streaking through campus (like you haven't done worse), Pennyfeather ends up as the head of a boys' school in Wales, where he becomes engaged to a wealthy sugar mommy—whose cash secretly comes from the South American brothel industry. Get lost in your own Peruvian bordello with help from pisco, a South American grape brandy that pairs fast and fun with standard cola.

2 ounces pisco
1 (12-ounce) can cola

Pour the pisco over ice in a highball glass and fill to the top with the cola. These go down so quick, you could end up half naked and quacking on the quad.

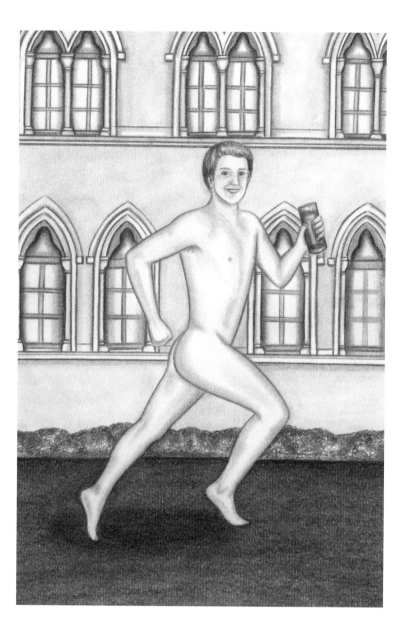

DRANKENSTEIN

FRANKENSTEIN (1818)
BY MARY SHELLEY

Mary Shelley created more than a monster when she anony-mously published *Frankenstein* at age twenty-one—she also birthed one of pop culture's greatest misattributions: Frankenstein is the name of the whacko doctor, *not* the green-faced, peg-necked creature. (He gets his own nicknames, including "vile insect" and "wretched devil," courtesy of his dear old dad.) Experiment with the following Halloween-ready, bright green concoction. Heads up: more than a few couples have played their own version of doctor after downing more than a few of these.

   1 ounce melon liqueur
   1 ounce tequila
   1 (12-ounce) can club soda

Pour the liqueur and tequila over ice in a highball glass, then fill to the top with the club soda. Now, light a few candles, lock the door, and guard your potion with monosyllabic grunts.

HUCKLEBERRY SIN

ADVENTURES OF HUCKLEBERRY FINN (1884)
BY MARK TWAIN

Conceived to exploit the success of the author's earlier, blatantly comic *The Adventures of Tom Sawyer*, *Huck Finn* emerged as a stand-alone classic. In folksy first person, Huck recounts riverboat escapades, narrow escapes, and occasional cross-dressing, set against a Mississippi River raging with racial strife. Mark Twain—a pen name riff on safety measurements used for steamboats—intended the book as an excoriating critique of slavery, but to this day it remains banned in some libraries across our lands, with parents and teachers crying (irony alert!) racism. Drink the tension away with a bittersweet tribute to Huck's pap, a daylight drunk who could've used a good education.

 5 fresh blueberries, washed
 2 ounces berry-flavored vodka (like 44° North Mountain
     Huckleberry Flavored Vodka)
 1 (12-ounce) can club soda

Muddle the blueberries in the bottom of a mason jar. Add ice and pour in the vodka, filling to the top with the club soda. Enjoy the sunset—but stay alert for riverbank beverage bandits.

ABSINTHE SHRUGGED

ATLAS SHRUGGED (1957)
BY AYN RAND

I f you suffer from debilitating back pain, odds are you either
exercise incorrectly, don't exercise at all, or once tried to get
through *Atlas Shrugged*. Ayn Rand's heavier-than-a-toddler
dystopian novel, in which much of the general public turns against
mounting government regulations, remains a controversial slog
today. Why not match this big boy with a similarly shifty ingredient: absinthe. Legendary for its rumored hallucinogenic effects,
absinthe was banned in the U.S.A. in 1962, but recently reemerged
as a kind of lovingly legal lighter fluid. Enjoy this debatable beverage tucked into your bunker with that aching back (and hulking
book), hiding from the rest of society.

1 ounce absinthe
1 sugar cube

Pour the absinthe into a rocks glass, lay a butter knife across
the rim, and balance the sugar cube on top. Slowly run
three to four ounces of ice-cold water over the cube and
into the rocks glass, allowing the mixture to cloud. Remove
the knife, retreat to the basement, and sip to your conspiracy
theorist's content.

THE COUNT OF MONTE CRISTAL

THE COUNT OF MONTE CRISTO (1844–45)
BY ALEXANDRE DUMAS

Alexandre Dumas knew a thing or two about keeping an audience tuned in. Heck, he knew a thing or *eighteen*, because that's how many newspaper installments it took to tell *The Count of Monte Cristo*, which still sets the bar for archetypical revenge tales. You know the protagonist's formula: (1) Get wrongfully convicted; (2) Go to jail; (3) Get out and get even. Oh yeah, and (4) Get *rich* along the way—the kind of rich that can fill a Jacuzzi with Champagne. Turn the bubbles up high and hop into our sweet-as-vengeance Cristal cocktail. Be warned: it could take prison-worthy deeds to snag the really pricey stuff.

> 1 ounce elderflower liqueur (like St-Germain)
> Champagne (like Cristal), to fill
>
> Pour the liqueur into your fanciest flute and top with the best bubbly you can buy. (And if you *can* afford Cristal? Lose the liqueur, double the good stuff, and—hold up—can you spot a dude a fifty?)

MOBY-DRINK

MOBY-DICK (1851)
BY HERMAN MELVILLE

This one'll make you think twice about flushing a goldfish down your toilet. In Melville's *Moby-Dick*, published first in England (and greeted with scathing reviews!), the titular whale is best known for attacking Captain Ahab's ship and then—talk about special skills—chewing off the poor fella's leg. Ahab spends the rest of his career limping around, determined to exact revenge on Moby-D, only to finally spear the whale and—Plan B!—get dragged underwater to his own ironic death. Our sea-inspired cocktail is as blue as the Pacific, but the real fun is in playing fish hunter. Grab a harpoon and get even.

1 ounce vodka
½ ounce Blue Curaçao
1 (12-ounce) can lemon-lime soda
1 Swedish Fish candy, for garnish

Combine the vodka and Blue Curaçao over ice in a highball glass and fill to the top with the lemon-lime soda. Now for the demonic part: grab that Swedish Fish by the gills, spear it with a swizzle stick, and get plunging. Just don't fall in yourself.

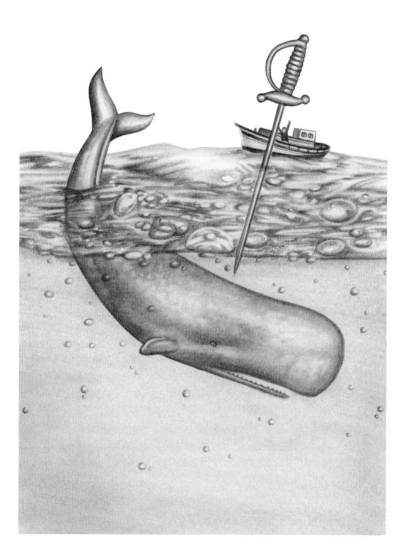

GULP-IVER'S TRAVELS

GULLIVER'S TRAVELS (1726)
BY JONATHAN SWIFT

Your grandparents knew *Gulliver's Travels* as a morality tale wrapped in droll travelogue: an Englishman lost at sea stumbles upon a handful of bizarre lands in which he is by turns the biggest and the smallest creature for miles, leading him to question everything from patriotism to religion to his very definition of home. *You* know *Gulliver's Travels* as the critically panned, audience-ignored film that featured Jack Black putting out a fire by peeing on it (hope you took off the 3-D glasses for that part). In our beachy keen nod to the hero washed ashore, choose your own adventure with a Lilliputian shooter or Brobdingnagian cocktail. Try saying *that* three times drunk.

½ ounce vodka
½ ounce peach schnapps
½ ounce grapefruit juice
½ ounce cranberry juice

Shake the ingredients with ice and strain into an empty rocks glass; this goes down in a single swig. For the bigger, Brobdingnagian variation on the above, double all ingredients, shake with ice, and strain into a cocktail glass. Little seasick? Eyes on the horizon, sailor.

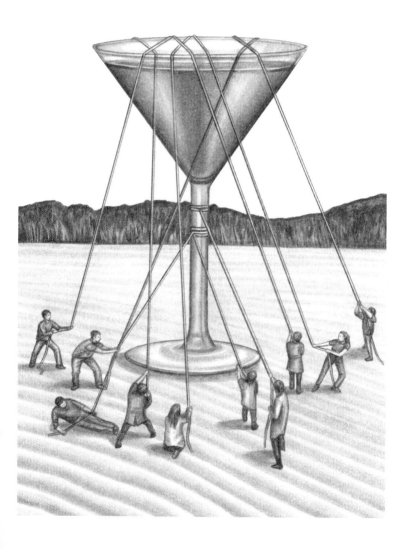

A CONFEDERACY of OUNCES

A CONFEDERACY OF DUNCES (1980)
BY JOHN KENNEDY TOOLE

Originally handwritten on piles of paper, *A Confederacy of Dunces* found life only after its author lost his own; John Kennedy Toole committed suicide, his mother found those secret pages, and she began hawking the thing around their home state of Louisiana, claiming it was the next great American novel. (Sorry, guys: sometimes moms are right.) Now a universally adored Pulitzer-winner starring a brilliant New Orleans nut with a heart of odd, this classic goes best with another: the Big Easy's own Sazerac. Raise a glass to the tragically shortchanged Toole—and everything else he might have written.

½ ounce anise liqueur (like Herbsaint)
1½ ounces rye whiskey
1 teaspoon sugar
3 dashes Peychaud's bitters
2 dashes Angostura bitters
Lemon twist, for garnish

Pour the liqueur into a chilled rocks glass, swirl around till the sides are nice and coated, and then toss anything that doesn't stick. Add the remaining ingredients to a shaker with ice, shake well, and strain into the glass. Guests? Lemon twist garnish. No guests? Cut the cute and get reading.

THE LAST OF THE MOJITOS

THE LAST OF THE MOHICANS (1826)
BY JAMES FENIMORE COOPER

Long before the universally adored film came out, *The Last of the Mohicans* was landmark (if historically wobbly) literature. Chronicling the tomahawk-assisted turf wars of Native Americans, Cooper stuffed his pages with wordy, witless plot-stoppers: "Duncan wandered among the lodges, unquestioned and unnoticed, endeavoring to find some trace of her in whose behalf he incurred the risk he ran," anyone? Anyone? We'll help you through the slow parts. Take a classic mojito and launch your own sneak attack, losing the sugar for agave nectar and adding a few authentically Native American fruits to the party. The result could stop wars.

> 5 fresh blueberries, washed
> 3 small, fresh strawberries, washed
> 8 sprigs fresh mint, washed
> ½ ounce lemon juice
> 1 ounce agave nectar
> 1½ ounces light rum
> 1 (12-ounce) can club soda

Muddle the berries, mint, juice, and nectar in a Collins glass. Add 2 handfuls ice and the rum, give a good stir, and top off with the club soda. Expect a rain dance of happy tears.

THE LIME OF THE

ANCIENT MARINER

THE RIME OF THE ANCIENT MARINER (1798)
BY SAMUEL TAYLOR COLERIDGE

Next time you're marooned on an island, resist the temptation to call out, "Water, water everywhere, and not a drop to drink!" First of all, the other survivors don't need a clever quote, they need cocktails and a grief counselor. Second, you'll probably end up dying of dehydration, so your final words ought to be accurate. The *actual* phrase—"Water, water everywhere, nor any drop to drink"—is from an epic poem about bad weather, angry oceans, and pissed-off dead birds who aren't afraid to haunt a hull. (Moral of the story: leave God's creatures alone, skipper.) Celebrate your land legs with this limey twist on a salty classic—and seriously consider staying back on the beach.

    Sea salt, for highball rim (page 7)
    2 ounces lime juice
    2 ounces grapefruit juice
    1½ ounces gin

    Rim a chilled highball glass in sea salt. Fill the glass with ice, pour in the ingredients, and give a good stir. When you're sobered up, matey, head back to the lookout deck— and watch out for low-flying birds.

LORD OF THE MAI-TAIS

LORD OF THE FLIES (1954)
BY WILLIAM GOLDING

T he plot that started a dozen TV franchises: throw a group of disparate souls on an island after their airplane crashes, and, in a Clearasil-ready twist, make sure none of them are old enough to drive, let alone drink. If you went to a high school that favored broadened minds over banned books, you'll remember devouring this fable of order and disorder, schoolboys-turned-savages, and one very trippy pig's head. Recommended reading during your next flight to Hawaii, escape to the galley if things get bumpy and throw together this Polynesian nerve-calmer. It's fit to be served in a conch shell, but don't turn your back on the other passengers.

- 2 ounces cranberry juice
- 2 ounces orange juice
- 1½ ounces light rum
- 1 ounce coconut rum
- 1 teaspoon grenadine syrup (page 11)
- Orange slice or pineapple wedge, for garnish (optional)

Shake the ingredients with ice—odds are, it'll *all* turn out bloody red—and pour everything, including the ice, into a Collins glass. Get creative with the tropical garnishes: pineapples, oranges, eye of piglet. . . .

INFINITE ZEST

INFINITE JEST (1996)
BY DAVID FOSTER WALLACE

A *Ten Commandments*—size cast populates this rule-breaking modern classic, infamous for sprawling prose, endless footnotes,[1] and a madcap depiction of the future.[2] Confounding and delightful in equal measure, *Jest* takes place in the 'burbs of Boston,[3] between a halfway house and a nearby tennis academy. Wallace had one of his central characters take his own life, and in a tragic true-life twist, Wallace did the same, leaving behind a magnum opus that will be argued and digested for infinity. Serve up a tennis-ball-yellow cocktail that mimics the zest and bounce of one fallen literary legend.

2 ounces vodka
1 ounce limoncello
½ ounce lemon juice

Minding that tennis elbow, shake the ingredients with ice and strain into a cocktail glass. Head back to the court, sport, and never give up on your game.

[1] Just like this, but they appeared at the end of the book—over four hundred of 'em!

[2] Time is marked with corporate sponsorships, as in Year of the Perdue Wonderchicken.

[3] Wallace briefly studied philosophy at Harvard (who *hasn't?*) and later taught at Emerson.

HEART OF DARK MIST

HEART OF DARKNESS (1899)
BY JOSEPH CONRAD

What is it with white guys and their imperialistic, waterborne adventures? Yet again, we encounter a Western classic that drops a "civilized" man (Charles Marlow of England) into the middle of a foreign land (the Congo wilds, which stand to be colonized). Things get sticky in the retelling: *Heart of Darkness* is as open to celebration as it is to question, with readers and critics wondering if it's a novel *about* prejudice . . . or just a prejudiced novel. (The natives don't even get dialogue!) Such themes are above our pay grade, so we'll just stick to asking the questions, leaving the room, and coming back with a drink as dark and misty as the awkward silence hanging around us.

1½ ounces blackberry liqueur
½ ounce gin
½ ounce lemon juice

As quickly as possible—the guests need you in the living room, and *for the love of God when did the music stop playing?*—shake all ingredients with ice and strain into a chilled cocktail glass.

THE **MOONSHINE** AND **SIXPENCE**

THE MOON AND SIXPENCE (1919)
BY W. SOMERSET MAUGHAM

H ell hath no midlife crisis like a stockbroker who wakes up one day, looks at his wife and kids at breakfast, and announces he's taking a one-way trip to Paris to pursue life as a painter. *Now could somebody please pass Daddy the pancakes?* Along the way, Maugham's artist—a stand-in for famed real-life painter Paul Gauguin—makes the perfectly logical geographical progression from Paris to Marseilles to Tahiti, where he finally finds contentment and his own kind of success (never mind his leprosy in the end). Sip on this "moonshine" cooler next time you need inspiration to break out of that cubicle and head to the tropics—even if only in your dreams.

1½ ounces cheap whiskey
Splash of pineapple juice
Squeeze of coconut cream (like Coco Reál Cream of Coconut)

Pour the ingredients over ice in a rocks glass (or travel mug!). Give a good stir, grab your *Tahitian for Dummies* guide, and head for the airport; you're goin' places.

A FAREWELL TO AMARETTO

A FAREWELL TO ARMS (1929)
BY ERNEST HEMINGWAY

Widely lauded as Hemingway's most accomplished work, *A Farewell to Arms* firmly established his spare, just-the-facts prose. Little wonder: before doing time as an ambulance driver in World War I, Hemingway was a junior reporter in Kansas City. Much of *Farewell* draws directly from Hemingway's own life abroad, from mortar shell injuries to angelic nurses. Nobody said war was easy, but just when you think the narrative is gonna land nice and quiet in Switzerland, Hemingway throws a friggin' dead *baby* into the mix. We salute Hemingway's complicated time in the Italian campaign with that country's own amaretto. Take this one like a soldier: sour but fighting.

2 ounces amaretto
½ ounce lemon juice
1 teaspoon granulated sugar

Combine the amaretto, lemon juice, and sugar in a shaker with ice. Shake well and strain over fresh ice in a rocks glass. Best enjoyed after returning home from a stint overseas, with bonus points awarded if you can get your girlfriend— or boyfriend!—into a nurse's uniform.

ONE HUNDRED BEERS

OF SOLITUDE

ONE HUNDRED YEARS OF SOLITUDE (1967)
BY GABRIEL GARCÍA MÁRQUEZ

T he most celebrated work by Latin America's prince of prose,
One Hundred Years of Solitude traces one family's multigenerational triumphs and devastations in establishing a South American
settlement. Pressing hard on the symbolism pedal, Márquez uses
the colors yellow and gold like a weaver, threading death and
wealth throughout a story of inevitable decline. We borrow his
palette, pairing South America's most famous beer—Cusqueña, the
"gold of Incas"—with a cheery, yellow lemonade. The result is so
lightweight, you can water your solitude down with a hundred of
these—give or take your dignity.

> 3 ounces carbonated lemonade
> (like Martinelli's Sparkling Classic Lemonade)
> 8 ounces light beer (like Cusqueña)
> 2 dashes Angostura bitters

Pour the lemonade into a chilled pint glass. Fill to the top
with beer and add a dash or two of bitters. Now, sit back
and prepare for life's ups and downs . . . you know, with
another drink standing by.

ORANGE JULIUS CAESAR

JULIUS CAESAR (CIRCA 1599)
BY WILLIAM SHAKESPEARE

F riends, Romans, upperclassmen: with pals like this, who needs enemies? Shakespeare's *Julius Caesar* reads like a luxuriantly extended definition of the word "backstabber," as the title character's rise in power inspires those closest to him to plot his assassination. Though Caesar gets top billing, he actually appears in only a handful of scenes; the real star here is Marcus Brutus, proving that sometimes a secondary player can walk away with the show. Sneak a little mother's milk into an old-fashioned breakfast recipe—and trust us (no, really, you can trust us), the result is pretty killer.

    3 ounces orange juice
    2 ounces milk
    1½ ounces light rum
    1 teaspoon granulated sugar
    ¼ teaspoon vanilla

Have your closest frenemy load all the ingredients, plus a handful of ice, into your blender. Only *after* he removes his fingers, get whirring. Serve in a Collins glass.

VERMOUTH THE BELL TOLLS

FOR WHOM THE BELL TOLLS (1940)
BY ERNEST HEMINGWAY

You'll *need* a drink for this one, a clench-jawed war classic that follows one Robert Jordan, an American abroad during the Spanish Civil War, and part of a daring underground mission to destroy an enemy's bridge. With a reporter's unflinching eye for the miseries of battle, Hemingway tells much of the novel in an English idiom that feels directly translated from Spanish, with a distractingly choppy narrative that's worth the slog (lest you miss the earth-moving sex scene midway through). You'll be a prisoner of *more* to our cocktail, featuring Spain's own sherry. Serve the result and you'll be building more bridges than you burn.

  2 ounces sherry
  1 ounce sweet vermouth
  Dash of Peychaud's bitters

Combine the sherry and sweet vermouth over ice in a rocks glass. Stir well and add the bitters. Serve to a longtime rival as a peace offering—and offer to take the first "poison control" sip.

SILAS MARNIER

SILAS MARNER (1861)
BY GEORGE ELIOT

Dude writes like a lady! Penned under the name "George Eliot,"
Mary Ann Evan's *Silas Marner* is the tale of a man wronged by
his church—closely mirroring the author's own disenchantment
with religion. It's only after Marner loses his gold fortune (only *after*
he's forced to leave town under false accusations of stealing from
his congregation's coffers) that he discovers his true idea of wealth:
becoming a father. Hailed as a clever critique of organized worship
and industrialized England, *Silas Marner* inspires a drink that's a little bitter and a little gold-flecked—sort of like a man's own life.

1 ounce Goldschläger
½ ounce Grand Marnier
1 (12-ounce) can ginger ale
3 dashes Angostura bitters

Combine the Goldschläger and Grand Marnier over ice in a
highball glass. Fill to the top with the ginger ale and add
bitters. Get ready for the next best thing to holy water.

THE OLD MAN AND THE SEAGRAM'S

THE OLD MAN AND THE SEA (1952)
BY ERNEST HEMINGWAY

A Pulitzer winner drowning in biblical allegory, *The Old Man and the Sea* was Hemingway's final published work in a career dripping with awards and accolades—and alcohol. The premise is simple (and familiar to readers of *Moby-Dick* and enjoyers of **Moby-Drink** on page 64): an old man sets out to destroy a fish in an act of single-minded delirium. During an epic three-day battle in which the marlin is finally defeated, hitched to the side of the boat, and—hey, old chum!—eaten by sharks en route to shore, the old man emerges weary but victorious. Do your best sailor imitation with the standby gear of any fisherman: whiskey and bait.

2 ounces whiskey (like Seagram's)
1 (12-ounce) can lemon-lime soda
Kumquat, for garnish

Warning: you're gonna need a bigger glass. Combine the whiskey and lemon-lime soda over ice in a highball glass. Grab some fishing tackle (looks like a fish; has a hook), give it a soapy scrubbing, and then bait 'n' float your kumquat. Alternatively, lose the glass and fill a fisherman's flask. Just don't sip and sail.

THE MALTED FALCON

THE MALTESE FALCON (1930)
BY DASHIELL HAMMETT

Unless you're a senior at P.D.U. (that's Private Detective University), ninety bucks says you skipped *The Maltese Falcon*, a popular pulpy novel that became a gun-for-gun film retelling with Humphrey Bogart as a cynical spy for hire. Though it may read like a series of stereotypes today, Dashiell Hammett's shady cast of femmes fatales and jewel thieves practically wrote the playbook for crime fiction—and the subsequent film noir boom it helped get off the ground. Speaking of which, our simple swill will have you flying higher than a falcon figurine. Slam with suspicion, 'cause this one goes down as gritty and unsentimental as any good private eye.

8 ounces malt liquor
1½ ounces butterscotch liqueur

Pour the malt liquor into a chilled pint glass, and the liqueur into a shot glass. Drop the entire shot, including the glass, into the malt liquor, and . . . uh . . . "enjoy." Now, watch the door and keep one finger on the metaphorical trigger. You're staying in for the night after one of these.

TWENTY THOUSAND LEAGUES
UNDER THE SEA BREEZE

TWENTY THOUSAND LEAGUES UNDER THE SEA (1870)
BY JULES VERNE

T ranslated, adapted, sometimes even copied (see: *Finding Nemo,* among others), this dazzling adventure by Jules Verne, the French father of science fiction, was shockingly prescient in its depiction of future underwater technologies. A time-tested tale of "Boy meets fish, fish turns out to be secret submarine, submarine never lets boy leave because *now he knows too much," Twenty Thousand Leagues* sends readers into chilly ocean depths, where they meet eccentric scientists, memorable sea monsters, and one very unforgiving whirlpool. Swirl up your grandfather's Sea Breeze recipe with a little carbonation—and settle old scores by serving this one with calamari.

1½ ounces vodka
2 ounces grapefruit juice
2 ounces cranberry juice
1 (12-ounce) can club soda

Combine the vodka and juices over ice in a highball glass, and fill to the top with the club soda. Drink slowly to avoid the bends—and come up for air every now and then, diver boy.

LORD PIMM

LORD JIM (1899)
BY JOSEPH CONRAD

I f it ain't broke, recycle your narrator. You remember Marlow, the complicated Englishman of Conrad's earlier *Heart of Darkness*? (Don't get too cocky, it was only ten recipes ago.) Marlow's baaaack, this time telling another man's tale. Jim is a young seaman who fancies himself a hero—only to abandon a ship full of Mecca-bound pilgrims when tragedy literally strikes. (Note: if you wanna make some serious coin, go back a hundred years and write about conflicted men at sea.) Told out of chronological order in an innovative, multi-narrator format, *Lord Jim* can nonetheless get a tad stuffy. Spice these Brits up with a famous English beverage that'll turn any host into a hero.

> 1 cucumber, sliced thin into wheels, including 1 wedge
>   for garnish
> 2 ounces Pimm's No. 1
> 1 (12-ounce) can lemon-lime soda
> Lemon wedge, for garnish

Place several cucumber wheels in a Collins glass, fill with ice, and pour in the Pimm's. Fill to the top with lemon-lime soda, squeeze and drop a lemon wedge into the glass, and garnish with a cucumber for serious cred. And for the love of Triton: serve women and childlike adults first.

THE SOUND AND THE SLURRY

THE SOUND AND THE FURY (1929)
BY WILLIAM FAULKNER

A southern family's tragic downfall told from three distinct voices—with a final, omniscient chapter—*The Sound and the Fury* became popular only after one of Faulkner's later novels took off. With unreliable narrators who zigzag between suicidal impulses, mental handicaps, *and an eye-crossing usage of italics*, this one may have helped earn its author a Nobel, but it's no beach read. Set in a fictional Mississippi town dealing with very factual post–Civil War growing pains, *The Sound* inspires a cocktail that hangs on furiously to a traditional southern recipe—because some things are best left unexamined.

2 ounces gin
½ ounce crème de cassis
½ ounce lemon juice

Shake the ingredients with ice and strain into a cocktail glass. Alternatively, serve on the rocks—just like your last family reunion.

BEVVIES
FOR
BOOK CLUBS

"Too much of anything is bad, but
too much Champagne is just right."
—Mark Twain

Uh-oh. Your turn to host that well-intentioned book club again?
Worried your idea of literature (Nicholas Sparks) might not live
up to the group's (*Nicholas Nickleby*)? Relax. Any of the following
time-tested classics should inspire both a hot debate and
a cool drink. Hell, die-hard Dewey decimal devotees can *always*
benefit from a little loosening up come critique time. After all, a
party can only stay seated for so long.

FAHRENHEIT 151

FAHRENHEIT 451 (1953)

BY RAY BRADBURY

It ain't about censorship, kids! Bradbury's then-futuristic *Fahrenheit 451* (the temperature at which a book burns) is about a ~~truly unthinkable~~ society in which technology reigns supreme and books go bye-bye. Written in the fifties but ringing eerily true today, *Fahrenheit's* world stars firemen who *start* the flames, setting the written word afire and sniffing out pesky, law-breaking readers. Serve up a burning-hot party drink to toast the peerless printed page—hey, you don't wanna spill rum on a Kindle. Soon as this one's ready to serve, disconnect the crock pot (and all your iGadgets) and reconnect with your party.

MAKES ABOUT 10 DRINKS

6 cups apple cider

1 cup cranberry juice

1 cup orange juice

1 cup pineapple juice

6 cloves

4 cinnamon sticks

8 ounces rum (like Bacardi 151)

Pour the ingredients, except the rum, into a crock pot. Warm for approximately 1 hour, or until heated through. *After* everyone has turned in their cell phones, unplug the pot and add the rum. Give it a stir and ladle away.

GONE WITH THE WINE

GONE WITH THE WIND (1936)
BY MARGARET MITCHELL

When Margaret Mitchell proclaimed that *Wind* was a story of survival, she was likely referring to her heroine, Scarlett O'Hara, who starts off a southern belle and ends up losing the hoop skirt to scavenge for food. You'll call yourself a survivor, too, when you get through the thousand-odd pages. A Pulitzer winner for the plucky Mitchell—her *second* marriage was to the best man at her *first* wedding—*Wind* is an enduring moneymaker. Gather a group, skip the movie, scour the book, and cool off a boiling discussion with this sangria: red as the earth of Tara and packed with proper Georgia peaches.

MAKES ABOUT 6 DRINKS
1 bottle red wine (about 3 cups)
2 ounces peach brandy
2 tablespoons sugar
1 peach, chopped into cute little squares
1 orange, cut into bite-size wedges
2½ cups ginger ale, chilled

Pour the wine, brandy, sugar, and fruits into a large pitcher and stir. Place the pitcher in the fridge and allow to infuse for at least an hour. When guests need a break—you'll know, because somebody will refer to Ashley as a girl; *this person did not read the book*—top the pitcher off with ginger ale and serve over ample ice. It's cool-down time.

THE RYE IN THE CATCHER

THE CATCHER IN THE RYE (1951)
BY J. D. SALINGER

The most celebrated work by a legendarily reclusive author, *The Catcher in the Rye* spoke directly to the disenchanted, angsty youth of the fifties—and still echoes vibrantly to first-time novelists who pray their coming-of-age protagonist will be favorably compared to Holden Caulfield. Narrating from a mental ward, Caulfield colorfully recounts his times in and out of prep school, chasing (and getting rebuffed by) prostitutes, while gaining bloody noses, enemies, and overnights on train station benches. Throw together a traditional Christmas punch for an untraditional Christmas story: much of *Catcher* takes place at the holidays, and this one ought to lift the spirits of your crankiest elf.

MAKES ABOUT 8 DRINKS
½ bottle (about 1½ cups) rye whiskey
4 ounces pineapple juice
2 ounces lemon juice
1 liter ginger beer

Add the whiskey and juices to a punch bowl with a big ol' hunk of ice (page 7). Stir in the ginger beer and gather your pals. Time to chase those blues away.

THE ADVENTURES OF
SHERBET HOLMES

THE ADVENTURES OF SHERLOCK HOLMES (1891–92)
BY SIR ARTHUR CONAN DOYLE

P ro-tip: "Elementary, my dear Watson" was never *exactly* spoken by Sherlock Holmes. Conan Doyle's beloved sleuth appeared on the big screen saying that phrase, but not on the page; he was too busy being the only detective who could crack a case from the comfort of his armchair. We take a tip from a lesser-known story that appeared alongside twelve others in a blazingly popular magazine series: raise a glass to "The Blue Carbuncle," a Holmes whodunit involving a goose with a very expensive gem lodged very inconveniently in its neck. After you trade jewels for berries, the only remaining mystery will be why you've never made this party pleaser before.

MAKES ABOUT 10 DRINKS
1 quart berry sherbet
1 bottle (about 3 cups) Champagne, chilled
1 liter ginger ale
½ cup fresh blueberries, washed, for garnish

Empty the sherbet into a punch bowl and pour the Champagne and ginger ale on top. Float the blueberries and serve. Don't leave the room for long—you'll return to a fast-empty bowl and a classic whodrunkit.

THE PITCHER OF
DORIAN GREY GOOSE

THE PICTURE OF DORIAN GRAY (1890)
BY OSCAR WILDE

Boy, did this book have it all: knife fights, magic paintings, and (spoiler alert!) people who never age. Wilde wasn't just ahead of the cosmetic surgery boom here—he also pushed the envelope on homoeroticism, resulting in widespread censorship in later versions of the book. Try getting your hands on the juicy early copies of *Dorian*, and then gather a group of aging beauty queens (or simply aging queens), who'll be guaranteed to love our hedonistic youth serum. Just keep them away from your expensive art.

MAKES ABOUT 8 DRINKS
10 sprigs fresh mint, washed
1 (12-ounce) can frozen lemonade concentrate
2 cups vodka (like Grey Goose)
Cucumber, sliced into wheels, for garnish

Tear the mint, then place in the pitcher. Add the lemonade concentrate and stir until thawed. Pour in the vodka and 3 cups cold water and stir. Serve over ice, garnish with the cucumber wheels, and remember: age before beauty—if anyone will fess up.

THE PORTRAIT OF A PINK LADY

THE PORTRAIT OF A LADY (1880–81)
BY HENRY JAMES

A woman's liberty is at the pink, beating heart of Henry James's transatlantic novel, one of his finest in a life measured in words rather than women (James was an avowed celibate). Of course, Victorian-era independence is different from Victoria's Secret–era independence, and rather than go sad and single, the heroine chooses the *least* terrible suitor she can find and ends up wealthy, wed—and woeful. Our variation on a classic cocktail is best served to a group of ladies holding out for Mr. Right—or even just plain *right*—no matter how many sweethearts they may have to sift through.

MAKES ABOUT 12 DRINKS
1 liter gin
3 cups pink lemonade
6 ounces grenadine syrup (page 11)
1 liter club soda

Combine the ingredients, except the club soda, in a big punch bowl. Show off a little by adding one of those big, glamorous blocks of ice (page 7). Stir in the bubbles and sip away the troubles; the grass is always pinker on the other side of this cocktail.

THE JOY LUCK CLUB SODA

THE JOY LUCK CLUB (1989)
BY AMY TAN

A h, legacy. If you've heard Grandma tell the story of the first time she ever saw your Pap Pap, huddled with his doofy cadets on the other side of the dance hall, his eyes planted firmly on Grandma's ample bosom . . . come to think of it, Pap Pap was a perv. Point is, Amy Tan's multigenerational Chinese saga—recounted by a veritable family reunion of narrators—is one that anyone with a verbose relative can relate to. Nothing gets a story primed like a pair of loose lips. Pull out those war photos and get busy mixing up this variation on a popular Chinese restaurant standby, sweet as a fortune cookie and twice as lucky.

MAKES ABOUT 4 DRINKS
1½ cups light rum
1½ cups orange juice
½ cup club soda
¼ cup lemon juice
2 ounces brandy
2 ounces orgeat syrup

Add the ingredients, plus two handfuls ice, to a festive bowl. Grab four straws and get gabbing—perhaps finally asking Pap Pap how Grandma got the nickname "Anytime Alice." Actually . . . perhaps not.

4

REFRESHMENTS

FOR

RECOVERING READERS

> "Always do sober what you said
> you'd do drunk. That will teach
> you to keep your mouth shut."
> —Ernest Hemingway

Every group needs a designated driver, but sometimes even a hard-core hooch hound feels like taking it a little easy. In this section, we pulled our most beloved kid-lit classics off the shelf, figuring simpler times call for simpler addictions. Whether for hangovers or just hangouts, these nonalcoholic drinks are a tribute to the kinds of stories that hold up so beautifully, you'll want to reread them with totally clear eyes. Pull the covers over your head and grab a flashlight, a friend, and a handful of ice cubes. And then? Lights out!

CHARLIE AND THE

CHOCOLATE FAKE-TINI

CHARLIE AND THE CHOCOLATE FACTORY (1964)
BY ROALD DAHL

T he book that made us all long for our own golden ticket, *Charlie and the Chocolate Factory* was Roald Dahl's triumphant tribute to treats. Featuring an enigmatic chocolatier who has captured England's attention, *Charlie* finds five children, including our title character, winning a lucky pass inside the secret dessert lair, where the walls are lickable and the workers are orange (in early editions, Dahl's Oompa-Loompas were black pygmies, which didn't go over so hot with critics). No problem: later editions got politically correct, just in time for grown-ups and children alike to embrace all things *Wonka*. Take a dip into a chocolate martini that loses the liquor, entirely suitable for curious kiddos—and their chaperones, too.

Cocoa powder, for cocktail rim (page 7)
1 Hershey's Kiss
1½ ounces chocolate syrup
1½ ounces light cream

Rim a chilled cocktail glass in cocoa powder. Drop a Hershey's Kiss on the bottom. Shake the remaining ingredients with ice and strain over the candy. Prepare for pure imagination.

PEAR THE WILD THINGS ARE

WHERE THE WILD THINGS ARE (1963)
BY MAURICE SENDAK

Widely considered *the* children's book of all time, *Where the Wild Things Are* is the fantastical story of one boy's giant imagination, turning time-out in his bedroom into a trip to an island kingdom—complete with canoes, monsters, and one humbled temper. Believe it or not, this Caldecott-winning contemporary classic was banned widely when it first debuted—apparently parents and librarians didn't take a shine to such an angry child protagonist—but the kids didn't listen, sending Sendak to the top of their reading piles. Tame your own wild night out (not to mention that monster headache) with a hangover cure that'll stand the test of time.

4 ounces pear juice
2 ounces lemonade
2 ounces ginger ale

Combine the pear juice and lemonade over ice in a highball glass, then add the ginger ale. Now slip on your wolf PJs, draw the shades, and nurse that brain back to earth.

THE **PHANTOM TOLLJUICE**

THE PHANTOM TOLLBOOTH (1961)
BY NORTON JUSTER

You'd think a fantasy this trippy woulda been written in the seventies. We all remember Milo, bored to tears with suburban life till a mystical tollbooth arrives in his bedroom. Milo hops into his toy car and drives on through, ending up in the Land of Doldrums (and you thought the Midwest was a yawn). He's not there long, because there are maps to ignore, damsels to rescue, and clock-hawking hounds to befriend. Take your own trip back to summer camp, the boredom-busting destination where a mysterious "bug juice" has been served for eons. Reverse the clock with a color-changing cocktail that trades spirits for spirit.

MAKES ABOUT 8 DRINKS
1 packet powdered juice drink (like Kool-Aid, any flavor)
½ cup sugar
1 liter club soda
Lime, chopped into wedges, for garnish

Mix the Kool-Aid and sugar in a quart of water, then freeze in an ice cube tray. Empty the frozen cubes into cups, top with the club soda, and garnish with the lime wedges. Alternatively, go one cup at a time and save the rest of the cubes for later. Sometimes the best escapes are of the solo (or Solo cup) variety.

RIP VAN DRINKLE

"RIP VAN WINKLE" (1819)
BY WASHINGTON IRVING

A rare classic you can read in a single trip to the john, this short story packs a tall tale. In "Rip Van Winkle," one town's most lovable loner escapes his wife's nagging by setting off on foot into the Catskills, a mountainous New York region that the then-bankrupt English author had never even visited—and this was pre-Google! Van Winkle happens upon a group of folks bowling in the woods (don't ask), enjoys a sip from their mysterious keg, and ends up taking a very satisfying nap. Like, twenty *years* satisfying. Appearing in the same volume as "The Legend of Sleepy Hollow" (remember the Headless Horseman?), "Rip" inspires a naptime-inducing drink that'll have you nodding off before even *entertaining* the thought of outdoor exercise.

Chamomile tea bag
Kiwi wheel, peeled
Honey, to taste

Brew one mug of tea and add the kiwi—known for its sleep-inducing properties—and as much honey as your wandering heart longs for. This drink is so soothing, you might want to set an alarm first.

CHERRY POPPINS

MARY POPPINS (1934)
BY P. L. TRAVERS

An American favorite about a British nanny written by an Australian novelist. We all fell in love with Julie Andrews in the movie—and picked up a *terrible* Cockney accent from chimney-sweeping Dick Van Dyke—but this legend originated as a series of kids' books. Starring a stern but winking flying au pair, *Mary Poppins* understood tough love before daytime TV brought it into your mom's living room. We celebrate with a nod to Mary's home turf, Number Seventeen Cherry Tree Lane. This milkshake goes down so sweet, you won't even need a dash of sugar—let alone a spoonful.

1 scoop cherry frozen yogurt
4 ounces vanilla cream soda
5 maraschino cherries, plus 2 ounces of juice from jar
Splash of milk

Throw the ingredients into a blender with a handful of ice. Blend to desired consistency and serve in either a milkshake or a pint glass. For the love of Mary, make sure to garnish with an umbrella. Preferably black.

WHITE TANG

WHITE FANG (1906)
BY JACK LONDON

G ood vs. evil; man vs. man; wolf vs. dog. In *White Fang*—
which you should *not* take on a camping trip—a pack of
wolves polish off a couple of dogs before enjoying said dogs'
owner for dessert. Tracking the journey of White Fang, the
dog-with-a-touch-of-wolf's-blood hero, this quick read explores
what makes an animal (or man) truly wild, and how we all take
responsibility for bringing out the killer in each other. One easy
rule for a wintry hike: whether you're tame or not, never eat
yellow snow—unless it comes in the form of our frosty, canine-
inspired drink.

2 tablespoons Tang powder
3 ounces milk

Pour the Tang, 5 ounces of water, milk, and a handful of ice
cubes into a blender. Blend until smooth and serve in a
Collins glass. Drink this one fast enough and you're bound
to foam at the mouth.

PAT THE TUMMY

PAT THE BUNNY (1940)
BY DOROTHY KUNHARDT

Back when interactive meant reaching out and (novel concept, here) actually *touching* something, *Pat the Bunny* hopped onto the scene with wholesome, scratch-and-feel pages. Remember the sandpaper scruff on the dad? Or playing peek-a-boo with Paul (who was, frankly, too old to be playing peek-a-boo)? This quiet book made a loud dent, selling millions of copies and inspiring dolls, DVDs, and (don't pat *too* hard) even an app. We present a simple drink for long-gone times, back when a tummy ache would send you running to the nurse's office. Get back in the sandbox with one of these.

2 bags peppermint tea
3 slices fresh ginger

Place the tea bags and ginger slices in a tall mug. Fill the mug with hot water and allow it to steep for 10 minutes. Let it cool, then pour over ice in a highball glass. Rest that weary belly—and then it's time to get bouncing again.

On a boring note: raw ginger should not be consumed by children under two.

THE **WONDERFUL**

BLIZZARD OF **OZ**

THE WONDERFUL WIZARD OF OZ (1900)
BY L. FRANK BAUM

A poppy culture legend! If your knowledge of Dorothy (and her little dog, too) extends no further than the perennial classic film, you ought to take a look at the book that began it all—lest you miss the spicy stuff (killer bees; a crow-murdering Scarecrow) that didn't make it to the silver screen. Baum intended the novel as a one-time effort, but his publishers basically printed cash with his *Wonderful* words, and fourteen books in all appeared over twenty years. Follow your heart, freeze your brain, and have the courage to create a drink fit for a good witch: yellow as a brick road and swirly as a twister.

5 ounces pineapple juice
2 ounces coconut cream (like Coco Reál Cream of Coconut)
1 banana

Add the ingredients, plus a handful of ice, to a blender. Blend until smooth, and pour into a rocks or highball glass. Now, click your heels—or glasses—three times.

BAR BITES

FOR

BOOK HOUNDS

"One cannot think well, love well,
sleep well, if one has not dined well."
—Virginia Woolf

Hungry for something more substantial than even the most heavily garnished drink can deliver? You've come to the right place. When you're ready for a midpoint refuel from that shoulder-strainer of a book, try your hand at the following snacks. Grade-school treats disguised as grown-up eats, these bookish bar bites are fabulous for finicky guests and solo readers alike. Caution: this section may contain nuts—and that's just the protagonists.

ALICE'S ADVENTURES

IN WONDER BREAD

ALICE'S ADVENTURES IN WONDERLAND (1865)
BY LEWIS CARROLL

Difficult to believe, but when Charles Dodgson's (aka Lewis Carroll's) *Alice* debuted, critics derided the bunny-chasing, hookah-puffing storyline as utter nonsense. Ah, *critics*: that was the point—and Carroll's enchanted world became inspiration for myriad films, musicals, and spinoffs. Bite into our mushroom treat, just like Carroll's daring darling might have. It might not make you taller, but it'll certainly leave you grinning like a Cheshire cat.

MAKES 1 SANDWICH

½ tablespoon olive oil
10 cremini mushrooms (about ¼ pound), roughly chopped
Garlic salt and pepper, to taste
2 slices white bread (like Wonder Bread)
½ cup shredded Swiss cheese

Heat the olive oil in a skillet. Add the 'shrooms and stir for 5 minutes. Sprinkle the garlic salt and pepper and remove from heat. On a plate or cutting board, top one bread slice with the cheese and add the warm mushrooms from the skillet. Scrape out any bits from the skillet and recoat with a little olive oil, returning to medium heat. Make a sandwich with your slices and cook each side for a few minutes until nice and toasty. And if anyone comes near your sandwich? Off with their heads!

THE DEVILED EGG
WEARS PRADA

THE DEVIL WEARS PRADA (2003)
BY LAUREN WEISBERGER

Hark! A movie version that actually ups the ante! Lauren Weisberger's roman à clef, allegedly paralleling her time as assistant to *Vogue* editor-in-*charge* Anna Wintour, was a dishy phenomenon, strutting to the top of the *New York Times* bestseller list for a nice long catwalk. Chick lit turned chick flick with megahit results, led by Meryl Streep's silver hair (and tongue) and Anne Hathaway in dumpy mode. Dress down this cocktail-party standby with model-skinny ingredients and Prada-bright paprika flakes. Remember: every hall's a runway.

MAKES 12 SERVINGS
6 large eggs, hard boiled and peeled
1 (12-ounce) container of hummus
2 teaspoons lemon juice
½ teaspoon white vinegar
Salt and pepper, to taste
Paprika, for garnish

Insult the eggs until they fall to pieces, or just cut them lengthwise and remove their yellow-bellied innards. Toss out half the yolks, mash the rest in a bowl with hummus, lemon juice, and vinegar, and spoon it all back into the empty holes. Now, take the most attention-grabbing lipstick-red paprika you can find and go to town embellishing: you never know when someone's taking a picture.

OLIVES 'N' TWIST

OLIVER TWIST (1837–39)
BY CHARLES DICKENS

Charles Dickens knew his way around an empty belly: a one-time factory boy himself, Dickens was paid per *word* for his serialized novels, and *Oliver Twist* was an instant success with tabloid-hungry readers—even if critics called Dickens out for his shilling-seeking verbosity. Still, the adventures of a naive orphan who runs away, joins a gang of thieves, and ends up adopted by a wealthy family in the countryside remains good, if wordy, fun. Leave the gruel at the workhouse, because we're dressing up a college dorm appetizer in rich-kid clothes. Our lemon-twisted olives might compel your hungriest guests to beg for more, but this one's a cinch—and an Oliver-worthy steal.

MAKES 3 CUPS

3 cups mixed olives (all varieties)

2 teaspoons lemon zest

1 teaspoon olive oil

3 fresh rosemary sprigs

1 garlic clove, peeled and finely chopped

1 teaspoon dried red pepper flakes

Combine the ingredients in a jar or lidded container and give it a good shake—you've had enough practice after all these cocktails. For unexpected beggars at the door, serve in a bowl right away. Otherwise, keep this one in the fridge as a backup for lean times—provided those times arrive in the next couple of weeks.

FEAR OF FRYING

FEAR OF FLYING (1973) BY ERICA JONG

Have your mate and eat him, too! Erica Jong's controversial, woman-liberating seventies novel follows a nearly-thirty poet on an overseas trip with her second husband. Our gal Isadora is not a happy traveler, so she decides to "fly," indulging her wildest sexual longings—with a different man than she arrived with. Groundbreaking at the time, *Flying* may go down as soapy and self-obsessed, but it takes off as a rule-breaking, hear-me-soar manifesto. Lose none of your favorite chip's zip with our guiltless snack, coaxing kitchen newbies with just three ingredients—since two is never satisfying enough for anyone.

MAKES ONE "POPCORN BOWL" OF KALE
1 bunch kale (about 4 cups, packed)
2 tablespoons olive oil
Coarse salt, to taste

This is a good, crunchy snack after a bad, crunchy breakup. Take your head out of the oven and preheat to 375°F. Wash and pat dry the kale, tearing it into bite-size pieces and discarding the stems. Toss the kale with oil and salt in a medium bowl, and then arrange on a cooking sheet so the leaves don't touch one another. Bake for 15 to 20 minutes (nursing a bottle of white wine while you're at it) and remove from the oven. Let cool for 5 minutes—and start making the next batch. You're gonna *blow* through these, so to speak.

I KNOW THIS MUNCH IS TRUE

I KNOW THIS MUCH IS TRUE (1998) BY WALLY LAMB

No literary conversation (or recipe book, for that matter!) would be complete without a nod to lifestyle brand Oprah Winfrey, who came undone for this author's earlier work. By the time *I Know This Much Is True* landed on her book club rotation, Wally Lamb was a bookselling bonanza. *True* follows the histrionic exploits of a pair of twins, one of whom pulls a Van Gogh on his own hand, chopping the poor thing off in a library. A meditation on the shadowed, sad, and very Sicilian history of one family, this novel is also a battle cry for mental health care in this country. With apologies, you'll go nutty for a candied mix that'll spice up any family gathering—whether it needs it or not.

MAKES 4 CUPS
4 tablespoons (½ stick) salted butter
4 cups mixed pecans and cashews
2 teaspoons garlic salt
1 teaspoon ground pepper
½ teaspoon cayenne pepper
Pinch of light brown sugar

Melt the butter in a pan over medium heat, about 3 minutes. Add the nuts and stir to coat. Add the spices and sugar, continuing to stir until totally dissolved, and then lower your heat and let cook for 8 to 10 minutes, turning the nuts throughout. Remove from heat, allow to cool off, and transfer to a serving bowl. These are so easy to enjoy, you could eat 'em single-handed.

PIZZA AND WENDY

PETER AND WENDY (1911)
BY J. M. BARRIE

D isney don't own it! Peter Pan, the flying boy with *serious* growing-up issues (he crows like a rooster in public, among other things) is the brainchild of one J. M. Barrie, and was the inspiration for countless cartoons, recitals, and children breaking their ankles after leaping from their second-story windows. "All children, except one, grow up"—or maybe two, after you fix yourself this middle-school standby.

MAKES 2 MINI PIZZAS
1 English muffin, toasted and sliced in half
1 tablespoon marinara sauce
½ cup grated parmesan and provolone cheeses
Dried oregano, to taste

Spoon equal amounts of the marinara and cheese on your toasted English muffin slices. Top with the oregano, and microwave on high for 30 seconds to 2 minutes, depending on which war your appliances were manufactured after. Serve piping hot—and clap if you believe in easy snacks.

BERRY POTTER

HARRY POTTER AND THE SORCERER'S STONE (1997)
BY J. K. ROWLING

You haven't made it as an author till they've built a theme park around your phenomenon. First published in England—reportedly after seven publishers turned it down—*Harry Potter* leapt the pond to America before zooming around the world on a magic broomstick of success. A bona fide sensation, *Harry* introduced the world to new words (Muggles), sports (Quidditch), and billionaires (J. K. Rowling). Written when she was a broke single mum, Rowling's fantastical adventures eventually became the top-grossing film series of all time. Move over, Luke Skywalker, and make room for a classic British meringue as sweet and saucy as Rowling's delectable franchise.

MAKES 4 SERVINGS
4 cups fresh mixed berries (all varieties), washed
1 tablespoon granulated sugar
5 teaspoons pomegranate juice (like POM Wonderful)
½ ounce lemon juice
2 cups whipping cream
4 small store-bought meringues

Toss together the berries, sugar, and juices in a bowl, then set aside. Whip your cream in another bowl and crumble the meringue on top. Add half the berry mixture to the meringue-cream, folding over once. Dollop into four containers (ramekins or glass mugs work just fine) and top the whole affair off with the remaining berries. The result could have children (and adults) lined up around the block overnight.

PRAWN QUIXOTE

DON QUIXOTE (1605) BY MIGUEL DE CERVANTES

Quixotic, indeed: fed up with the lack of chivalry in his day and age—and this was the 1600s!—the retired Alonso Quijano changes his name to Don Quixote, throws on a suit of armor, and sets out for adventure with a fat sidekick and a model-thin horse. He meets whores, priests, and convicts, and if that sounds like a setup to a joke, you're right: *Don Quixote* is an elaborate romantic parody that, though written in two parts that were separated by a decade, is best consumed in one volume. Our classic shrimp cocktail gets a galloping-hot Spanish twist, with a result that's impossibly dreamy—and good fuel for your next quest.

MAKES 3 SERVINGS

½ cup ketchup

2 tablespoons horseradish

1½ ounces lemon juice

1 jalapeño pepper, seeded and diced

Salt and pepper, to taste

Hot sauce, to taste

10 to 15 fresh jumbo shrimp (about ½ pound),
   cooked and peeled

Cook the shrimp (or thaw according to the package directions, if frozen). Combine the ingredients, except the shrimp, in a small bowl, then spoon the sauce into three stemless wine glasses—you know, the kind that wobble all over the place. Arrange the shrimp artfully along the glass rims, and your guests will be tilting at windmills.

BONUS!

GAMES FOR GEEKS

DRINKING ALL BY YOUR LONESOME

Chug your ale each time Dickens introduces a new character in *Great Expectations*.

Pour a cold drink over your head every time you get an awkward boner during *Lolita*.

Take a sip of communion wine for every Biblical sin you've committed. Start at Genesis.

Do a shot each time you look over your shoulder during *1984*. Two shots if you get up to close the curtains.

Slam a Red Bull every time you turn the page in *Wuthering Heights*. Just to stay awake, actually.

Never *stop* **drinking** during *Flowers for Algernon*.

DRINKING WITH FRIENDS

Take turns trying to recite the infamous 11,282-word sentence from *Ulysses* in one breath. The person who stops first must drink most.

Get x copies of *The Shining* and x number of friends. In three rounds, race to find a specific word ("ax"; "hotel"; "scream"). The last to find each has to take a shot of (red) rum.

Smuggle booze into a library. Pull book titles out of the card catalog at random, playing "Never have I ever" with the classics: "Never have I ever read *The Great Gatsby*," etc. All who *have* read the book in question must take a swig from the bottle. Scholars get smashed.

Divide into teams. Lay a giant old edition of *The Canterbury Tales* open on a table. Take turns bouncing quarters, attempting to land them on top of the book. The losing team—that which lands the fewest quarters—must present a drunk oral report on *The Canterbury Tales* by dawn.

Trade off reading any of Shakespeare's short sonnets aloud. After your turn, try to explain—in plain English— what the Bard was actually attempting to say. The person most obviously bullshitting must move to England and open a pub.

Each already-tipsy participant reads a passage from *The Bell Jar* aloud. S/he who cries hardest must be cut off from alcohol immediately. It is suggested that the group embrace and then gently rock her/him.

FORMULAS FOR METRIC CONVERSIONS

Ounces to grams . . . . multiply ounces by 28.35

Pounds to grams . . . . multiply pounds by 453.5

Cups to liters . . . . multiply cups by .24

Fahrenheit to centigrade . . . . subtract 32 from Fahrenheit, multiply by 5, and divide by 9

METRIC EQUIVALENTS FOR VOLUME

U.S.	METRIC	
⅛ tsp.	0.6 ml	
¼ tsp.	1.2 ml	
½ tsp.	2.5 ml	
¾ tsp.	3.7 ml	
1 tsp.	5 ml	
1½ tsp.	7.4 ml	
2 tsp.	10 ml	
1 Tbsp.	15 ml	
1½ Tbsp.	22 ml	
2 Tbsp. (⅛ cup)	30 ml	1 fl. oz
3 Tbsp.	45 ml	
¼ cup	59 ml	2 fl. oz
⅓ cup	79 ml	
½ cup	118 ml	4 fl. oz
⅔ cup	158 ml	
¾ cup	178 ml	6 fl. oz
1 cup	237 ml	8 fl. oz
1¼ cups	300 ml	
1½ cups	355 ml	
1¾ cups	425 ml	
2 cups (1 pint)	500 ml	16 fl. oz
3 cups	725 ml	
4 cups (1 quart)	.95 liters	32 fl. oz
16 cups (1 gallon)	3.8 liters	128 fl. oz

OVEN TEMPERATURES

DEGREES FAHRENHEIT	DEGREES CENTIGRADE	BRITISH GAS MARKS
200°	93°	—
250°	120°	½
275°	140°	1
300°	150°	2
325°	165°	3
350°	175°	4
375°	190°	5
400°	200°	6
450°	230°	8

METRIC EQUIVALENTS FOR WEIGHT

U.S.	METRIC
1 oz	28 g
2 oz	57 g
3 oz	85 g
4 oz	113 g
5 oz	142 g
6 oz	170 g
7 oz	198 g
8 oz	227 g
16 oz (1 lb.)	454 g
2.2 lbs.	1 kilogram

METRIC EQUIVALENTS FOR BUTTER

U.S.	METRIC
2 tsp.	10 g
1 Tbsp.	15 g
1½ Tbsp.	22.5 g
2 Tbsp. (1 oz)	27 g
3 Tbsp.	42 g
4 Tbsp.	56 g
4 oz. (1 stick)	110 g
8 oz. (2 sticks)	220 g

METRIC EQUIVALENTS FOR LENGTH

U.S.	METRIC
¼ inch	.65 cm
½ inch	1.25 cm
1 inch	2.50 cm
2 inches	5.00 cm
3 inches	6.00 cm
4 inches	8.00 cm
5 inches	11.00 cm
6 inches	15.00 cm
7 inches	18.00 cm
8 inches	20.00 cm
9 inches	23.00 cm
12 inches	30.50 cm
15 inches	38.00 cm

Source: Herbst, Sharon Tyler. *The Food Lover's Companion*.
3rd ed. Hauppauge: Barron's, 2001.

ACKNOWLEDGMENTS

....

Loud, slurring thanks to my first drinkers and readers: the Federles (Andy and Marci; Dennis and Debbie; Mike and Lynne), Brian Elliot, Cheri Steinkellner, Christian Trimmer, Karen Katz, and Victoria D'amato-Moran.

Three cheers to Josh McDonnell and Lauren Mortimer on the knockout design and illustrations throughout.

A glass of rosé—even if we're in public—for Brenda Bowen, agent and all-around chief.

And ninety-nine bottles of beer *off* the wall for Jordana Tusman, editor and ally. Thank you for getting this book and for *getting* this book.

INDEX

D

E

F

G

....

Y

....